3-MINUTE LENT DAILY DEVOTIONAL 2024

Scripture Readings, Prayers, and Reflections to Nurture Your Faith During the Lenten Season and Easter 2024

BY

JOEL PRINTS

3-MINUTE LENT DAILY DEVOTIONAL 2024

Table of contents

3-MINUTE LENT DAILY DEVOTIONAL 2024

3-MINUTE LENT DAILY DEVOTIONAL 2024

3-MINUTE LENT DAILY DEVOTIONAL 2024

INTRODUCTION

NURTURING FAITH DURING LENT

Welcome to the transformative journey of the "3-Minute Lent Daily Devotional 2024." In these pages, we embark on a spiritual pilgrimage that transcends the hustle of daily life, inviting you to devote just three minutes each day to nourish your soul during the sacred season of Lent.

Overview of the 3-Minute Lent Daily Devotional

This devotional is crafted with the understanding that our lives are filled with various commitments, and yet, even in the busyness, we can carve out a small sacred space for reflection. Each day's devotion is designed to be a brief oasis for your spirit, offering Scripture readings, heartfelt prayers, and reflective moments aimed at fostering a deeper connection with your faith.

Importance of Lent in the Christian Faith:

Lent is more than a season; it is a profound and intentional period of preparation and reflection for Christians worldwide. Rooted in the 40 days that Jesus spent fasting in the wilderness, Lent invites us to follow His example of self-discipline, repentance, and spiritual growth. It's a time to draw closer to God, examining our hearts, and redirecting our focus toward the ultimate sacrifice of Christ on the cross.

During Lent, Christians are called to engage in prayer, fasting, and acts of kindness, mirroring the journey of Jesus leading up to His crucifixion and, ultimately, His triumphant resurrection on Easter Sunday. The season serves as a spiritual reset, allowing us to reassess our priorities and deepen our relationship with God.

As we delve into the pages of this devotional, may the significance of Lent unfold in your heart, leading to a transformative experience that transcends the 40 days and echoes throughout the entire year. Embrace the spiritual rhythm of Lent as we explore Scripture, join in prayer, and reflect on the profound love that culminates in the Easter celebration.

LENTEN SEASON BASICS

A Journey into Spiritual Renewal

Understanding Lent:
Lent is a sacred season in the Christian calendar, a period of approximately 40 days dedicated to spiritual reflection, repentance, and preparation for the joyous celebration of Easter. It symbolically mirrors Jesus Christ's 40 days of fasting and prayer in the wilderness. As we engage in Lent, we intentionally create space in our lives to draw closer to God, seeking a deeper understanding of our faith and a renewal of our spiritual commitment.

Historical Significance:
The roots of Lent trace back to the early Christian church, evolving over centuries into the observed tradition we recognize today. The 40-day duration corresponds to several biblical events, such as the

Israelites' 40 years of wandering and, most significantly, Jesus' 40 days of temptation in the wilderness. This period holds historical and theological importance, serving as a time of self-examination, repentance, and preparation for the Easter celebration of Christ's resurrection.

During the Middle Ages, Lent became more formalized as a season of penance and fasting. The practice of giving up certain luxuries or indulgences during this time serves as a tangible expression of solidarity with Christ's sacrifice and a reminder of our dependence on God.

Duration and Purpose:
Lent typically spans 40 days, excluding Sundays, representing the time Jesus spent in the wilderness. It begins on Ash Wednesday and concludes on Holy Saturday, the day before Easter Sunday. This intentional timeframe allows Christians to reflect on their lives, aligning their actions and attitudes with the teachings of Christ.

The purpose of Lent extends beyond mere ritual; it's a spiritual journey aimed at personal and communal growth. Fasting, prayer, and acts of kindness during this season are not meant as burdens but as vehicles for drawing nearer to God. Through self-denial and intentional reflection, we cultivate a deeper awareness of our spiritual needs and the transformative power of God's grace.

May this exploration into the Lenten season deepen your understanding, fostering a sense of purpose and renewal in your faith journey. Embrace the ancient practices with a contemporary heart, allowing Lent to be a transformative season of spiritual rediscovery.

PREPARING FOR LENT 2024

Cultivating a Sacred Pathway

Setting Spiritual Goals:
As we stand on the threshold of Lent 2024, consider this a moment to set intentional spiritual goals. These are not resolutions in the conventional sense but rather aspirations that align with the essence of Lent—drawing closer to God. Reflect on areas of your spiritual life that could benefit from growth, whether it be deepening prayer, practicing gratitude, or cultivating a spirit of forgiveness. By setting these goals, you invite God to work in transformative ways during this sacred season.

Creating a Devotional Space:
The physical environment in which you engage with God matters. Create a sacred space, a haven for your soul amidst the busyness of life. Whether it's a quiet corner with a comfortable chair, a candle, and a Bible, or a serene outdoor spot, let this space be a refuge for prayer and reflection. By intentionally

carving out this devotional space, you signal to yourself and to God your commitment to a dedicated time of spiritual nourishment during Lent.

Choosing Prayer and Reflection Tools:
Selecting the right tools can enhance your Lenten journey. Consider incorporating a daily devotional guide that aligns with your spiritual goals. Choose a Bible translation that resonates with you, and perhaps explore supplementary resources such as reflective journals or spiritual literature. Embrace prayer practices that speak to your heart—whether it's contemplative prayer, intercession, or gratitude prayers. The tools you choose should resonate with your unique spiritual journey, aiding you in staying focused and engaged throughout the season.

As you prepare for Lent 2024, remember that this is not a checklist to complete but a pathway to walk. Approach it with an open heart, allowing God to guide your goals, fill your sacred space with His presence, and speak to you through the chosen tools of prayer and reflection. May this preparation be a sacred beginning, setting the tone for a transformative Lenten season.

Day 1

A Foundation of Hope

Scripture Reading: Psalm 42:1-2 - "As the deer pants for streams of water, so my soul pants for you, my God. My soul thirsts for God, for the living God. When can I go and meet with God?"

PRAYERS : Heavenly Father, on this first day of our Lenten journey, I thirst for You. May my soul pant for Your presence, drawing me closer to the living God. Open my heart to the transformative power of this season.

Reflection for Spiritual Growth: Consider the depths of your spiritual thirst. How can you intentionally seek God's presence throughout this Lenten journey?

Daily Challenge and Action: Reach out to someone in need today. Your act of kindness becomes a ripple of hope in someone else's life.

Day 2

Embracing Humility

Scripture Reading: Philippians 2:3-4 - "Do nothing out of selfish ambition or vain conceit. Rather, in humility, value others above yourselves, not looking to your own interests but each of you to the interests of the others."

PRAYERS : Lord, instill in me a spirit of humility. Help me value others above myself and consider their needs. May my actions reflect the selfless love of Christ.

Reflection for Spiritual Growth: Reflect on areas in your life where humility can bring about positive change. How can you emulate Christ's humility in your interactions?

Daily Challenge and Action: Perform an anonymous act of kindness today, putting the needs of others before your own.

Day 3

Seeking Forgiveness

Scripture Reading: 1 John 1:9 - "If we confess our sins, he is faithful and just and will forgive us our sins and purify us from all unrighteousness."

PRAYERS : Gracious Father, I come before you, acknowledging my shortcomings. Grant me the courage to confess my sins and experience the cleansing power of Your forgiveness.

Reflection for Spiritual Growth: Reflect on the freedom that comes from seeking and receiving God's forgiveness. How can you extend this grace to others in your life?

Daily Challenge and Action: Initiate a conversation with someone you may have conflicts with and seek reconciliation. Extend the forgiveness you've received.

Day 4

Cultivating Gratitude

Scripture Reading: Psalm 136:1 - "Give thanks to the Lord, for he is good. His love endures forever."

PRAYERS : Heavenly Father, today I choose gratitude. Help me recognize Your goodness in every circumstance, and may my heart overflow with thanks for Your enduring love.

Reflection for Spiritual Growth: Reflect on the blessings in your life, both big and small. How can a spirit of gratitude deepen your connection with God during this Lenten season?

Daily Challenge and Action: Keep a gratitude journal. Write down three things you're thankful for each day, cultivating a habit of recognizing God's goodness.

Day 5

Surrendering Control

Scripture Reading: Proverbs 3:5-6 - "Trust in the Lord with all your heart and lean not on your own understanding; in all your ways submit to him, and he will make your paths straight."

PRAYERS : Heavenly Father, I surrender control of my life to You. Grant me the faith to trust Your wisdom and guidance, knowing that Your plans are higher than my own.

Reflection for Spiritual Growth: Reflect on areas where you struggle to let go of control. How can trusting God more deeply impact your peace and well-being?

Daily Challenge and Action: Identify one aspect of your life where you tend to take control. Purposefully release control and entrust it to God through prayer.

Day 6

Cultivating Compassion

Scripture Reading: Colossians 3:12 - "Therefore, as God's chosen people, holy and dearly loved, clothe yourselves with compassion, kindness, humility, gentleness, and patience."

PRAYERS : Lord, help me embody compassion today. Clothe me with kindness, humility, gentleness, and patience, reflecting Your love to those around me.

Reflection for Spiritual Growth: Consider ways you can actively demonstrate compassion in your daily interactions. How can your actions mirror God's love for others?

Daily Challenge and Action: Reach out to someone in need or offer a listening ear to a friend. Practice compassion in a tangible way.

Day 7

Embracing Silence

Scripture Reading: Psalm 46:10 - "Be still, and know that I am God; I will be exalted among the nations, I will be exalted in the earth."

PRAYERS : In the stillness, I seek Your presence, O Lord. Quiet my heart and mind, that I may know You more deeply and find rest in Your sovereignty.

Reflection for Spiritual Growth: Reflect on the role of silence in your spiritual life. How can intentional moments of stillness deepen your connection with God?

Daily Challenge and Action: Dedicate at least 10 minutes today to sit in silence, allowing your soul to rest in God's presence.

Day 8

Fostering Patience

Scripture Reading: James 5:7-8 - "Be patient, then, brothers and sisters, until the Lord's coming. See how the farmer waits for the land to yield its valuable crop, patiently waiting for the autumn and spring rains. You too, be patient and stand firm, because the Lord's coming is near."

PRAYERS : Lord, grant me patience as I wait on Your timing. Help me trust in Your promises, knowing that Your plans unfold in perfect precision.

Reflection for Spiritual Growth: Reflect on areas in your life where impatience may hinder your spiritual journey. How can embracing patience deepen your trust in God's timing?

Daily Challenge and Action: Practice patience in a specific situation today, trusting that God's timing is perfect.

Day 9

Cultivating Generosity

Scripture Reading: 2 Corinthians 9:7 - "Each of you should give what you have decided in your heart to give, not reluctantly or under compulsion, for God loves a cheerful giver."

PRAYERS : Lord, instill in me a heart of generosity. Guide my giving, not out of obligation but with joy and a cheerful spirit.

Reflection for Spiritual Growth: Reflect on the joy of giving and the impact it has on your spiritual well-being. How can generosity be a source of blessing for both the giver and the receiver?

Daily Challenge and Action: Find a way to be generous today, whether through a kind gesture, a thoughtful gift, or supporting a cause dear to your heart.

Day 10

Seeking Wisdom

Scripture Reading: Proverbs 2:6 - "For the Lord gives wisdom; from his mouth come knowledge and understanding."

PRAYERS : Heavenly Father, grant me Your wisdom. Open my heart to receive knowledge and understanding from You, that I may walk in Your ways.

Reflection for Spiritual Growth: Reflect on the value of seeking wisdom in your daily decisions. How can incorporating God's wisdom into your life enhance your spiritual journey?

Daily Challenge and Action: Face a decision today with prayer and seek God's wisdom before taking action.

Day 11

Embracing Gracious Speech

Scripture Reading: Colossians 4:6 - "Let your conversation be always full of grace, seasoned with salt, so that you may know how to answer everyone."

PRAYERS : Lord, guide my words today. May my speech be filled with grace and seasoned with the love that reflects Your character.

Reflection for Spiritual Growth: Reflect on the impact of your words on others. How can gracious speech foster a positive and Christ-like atmosphere in your interactions?

Daily Challenge and Action: Be intentional about using words of encouragement and grace in your conversations today.

Day 12

Nurturing Contentment

Scripture Reading: Philippians 4:11-12 - "I am not saying this because I am in need, for I have learned to be content whatever the circumstances. I know what it is to be in need, and I know what it is to have plenty. I have learned the secret of being content in any and every situation, whether well fed or hungry, whether living in plenty or in want."

PRAYERS : Heavenly Father, teach me the secret of contentment. Help me find peace and joy in You, regardless of my circumstances.

Reflection for Spiritual Growth: Reflect on areas in your life where contentment may be challenging. How can a grateful heart transform your perspective?

Daily Challenge and Action: Count your blessings today and express gratitude to God for the abundance in your life.

Day 13

Pursuing Holiness

Scripture Reading: 1 Peter 1:15-16 - "But just as he who called you is holy, so be holy in all you do; for it is written: 'Be holy, because I am holy.'"

PRAYERS : Lord, sanctify me and make me holy. Help me reflect Your character in all aspects of my life, striving for righteousness and purity.

Reflection for Spiritual Growth: Reflect on areas where God is calling you to greater holiness. How can your actions and choices align with God's standard of holiness?

Daily Challenge and Action: Identify one area of your life where you can make a conscious effort to live in accordance with God's holiness.

Day 14

Embracing Compassion for Yourself

Scripture Reading: Psalm 103:8 - "The Lord is compassionate and gracious, slow to anger, abounding in love."

PRAYERS : Lord, grant me the compassion to treat myself as You treat me—with love, grace, and understanding. Help me embrace Your forgiveness and move forward in faith.

Reflection for Spiritual Growth: Reflect on how God's compassion extends to you. How can you cultivate a compassionate and grace-filled attitude towards yourself?

Daily Challenge and Action: Practice self-compassion today, forgiving yourself for any shortcomings and embracing God's love.

Day 15

Connecting with God through Creation

Scripture Reading: Psalm 19:1 - "The heavens declare the glory of God; the skies proclaim the work of his hands."

PRAYERS : Creator God, as I observe Your creation, open my heart to experience Your glory. May the beauty of nature draw me closer to You.

Reflection for Spiritual Growth: Reflect on the wonders of God's creation. How can spending time in nature deepen your appreciation for the Creator?

Daily Challenge and Action: Spend time outdoors today, marveling at the beauty of God's creation and allowing it to inspire gratitude and awe.

Day 16

Resting in God's Presence

Scripture Reading: Exodus 33:14 - "The Lord replied, 'My Presence will go with you, and I will give you rest.'"

PRAYERS : Heavenly Father, grant me the rest that comes from abiding in Your presence. Help me find peace and solace in the assurance of Your company.

Reflection for Spiritual Growth: Reflect on the concept of rest in God's presence. How can you intentionally create moments of stillness to experience His peace?

Daily Challenge and Action: Dedicate a portion of your day to rest in God's presence through prayer, meditation, or simply being still.

Day 17

Expressing Joyful Gratitude

Scripture Reading: Psalm 100:4 - "Enter his gates with thanksgiving and his courts with praise; give thanks to him and praise his name."

PRAYERS : Lord, I enter Your presence with gratitude and joy. May my heart overflow with thanksgiving as I acknowledge Your goodness in my life.

Reflection for Spiritual Growth: Reflect on the joy that comes from expressing gratitude. How can cultivating a thankful heart enhance your spiritual journey?

Daily Challenge and Action: Express gratitude to God in a creative way today, whether through writing, art, or spoken words of thanks.

Day 18

Renewing the Mind

Scripture Reading: Romans 12:2 - "Do not conform to the pattern of this world but be transformed by the renewing of your mind. Then you will be able to test and approve what God's will is—his good, pleasing and perfect will."

PRAYERS : Lord, renew my mind and transform my thinking. Guide me away from worldly patterns, that I may align my thoughts with Your will.

Reflection for Spiritual Growth: Reflect on areas where your thinking may align with worldly patterns. How can renewing your mind contribute to a deeper understanding of God's will?

Daily Challenge and Action: Identify a negative thought pattern and intentionally replace it with a positive, God-centered perspective.

Day 19

Embracing Forgiveness

Scripture Reading: Ephesians 4:32 - "Be kind and compassionate to one another, forgiving each other, just as in Christ God forgave you."

PRAYERS : Gracious Father, help me embody forgiveness as You have forgiven me. Grant me the strength to extend grace to others, reflecting Your love.

Reflection for Spiritual Growth: Reflect on the power of forgiveness in your life. How can extending forgiveness contribute to your spiritual well-being?

Daily Challenge and Action: Extend forgiveness to someone who may have wronged you, releasing any lingering resentment.

Day 20

Trusting God's Plan

Scripture Reading: Jeremiah 29:11 - "'For I know the plans I have for you,' declares the Lord, 'plans to prosper you and not to harm you, plans to give you hope and a future.'"

PRAYERS : Lord, I trust Your plans for my life. Help me surrender my fears and anxieties, knowing that Your intentions are for my prosperity and hope.

Reflection for Spiritual Growth: Reflect on areas where trust in God's plan may be challenging. How can embracing His promises bring peace to your heart?

Daily Challenge and Action: Entrust a specific concern or worry to God today, acknowledging His sovereignty over your life.

Day 21

Growing in Humility

Scripture Reading: Philippians 2:3 - "Do nothing out of selfish ambition or vain conceit. Rather, in humility value others above yourselves."

PRAYERS : Lord, cultivate humility within me. Guide my actions to reflect a heart that values others above myself, just as Christ demonstrated.

Reflection for Spiritual Growth: Reflect on situations where humility may be lacking. How can embracing a humble attitude transform your relationships and interactions?

Daily Challenge and Action: Seek opportunities to serve others without seeking recognition or acknowledgment.

Day 22

Living in the Light of Truth

Scripture Reading: John 8:32 - "Then you will know the truth, and the truth will set you free."

PRAYERS : Heavenly Father, reveal Your truth to me. Set me free from falsehood and guide me in living a life aligned with Your Word.

Reflection for Spiritual Growth: Reflect on areas of your life where truth may be obscured. How can seeking and living in God's truth bring freedom?

Daily Challenge and Action: Commit to honesty in all your interactions today, seeking to live in the light of God's truth.

Day 23

Deepening Compassion for Others

Scripture Reading: Colossians 3:12 - "Therefore, as God's chosen people, holy and dearly loved, clothe yourselves with compassion, kindness, humility, gentleness, and patience."

PRAYERS : Lord, deepen my compassion for others. Clothe me with Your virtues, that I may mirror Your love to those around me.

Reflection for Spiritual Growth: Reflect on opportunities to show compassion. How can embodying God's virtues impact your relationships with others?

Daily Challenge and Action: Intentionally demonstrate compassion to someone in need today, extending kindness, humility, or patience.

Day 24

Seeking God's Guidance

Scripture Reading: Psalm 25:4-5 - "Show me your ways, Lord, teach me your paths. Guide me in your truth and teach me, for you are God my Savior, and my hope is in you all day long."

PRAYERS : Lord, guide me in Your ways and teach me Your truth. I place my hope in You, seeking Your guidance in every step of my journey.

Reflection for Spiritual Growth: Reflect on areas where you need God's guidance. How can seeking His direction bring clarity to your path?

Daily Challenge and Action: Before making a significant decision today, seek God's guidance through prayer and reflection.

Day 25

Cultivating a Heart of Worship

Scripture Reading: Psalm 95:1-2 - "Come, let us sing for joy to the Lord; let us shout aloud to the Rock of our salvation. Let us come before him with thanksgiving and extol him with music and song."

PRAYERS : Lord, I come before You with joy and thanksgiving. May my heart overflow with worship, acknowledging You as the Rock of my salvation.

Reflection for Spiritual Growth: Reflect on the role of worship in your life. How can cultivating a heart of worship deepen your connection with God?

Daily Challenge and Action: Engage in intentional worship today, whether through song, prayer, or contemplation, expressing gratitude and praise to God.

Day 26

Practicing Self-Discipline

Scripture Reading: 1 Corinthians 9:27 - "No, I strike a blow to my body and make it my slave so that after I have preached to others, I myself will not be disqualified for the prize."

PRAYERS : Lord, grant me self-discipline. Help me exercise control over my actions and desires, that I may live a life worthy of Your calling.

Reflection for Spiritual Growth: Reflect on areas of your life where self-discipline is needed. How can cultivating discipline lead to a more faithful and purposeful journey?

Daily Challenge and Action: Identify a habit or area that needs discipline in your life and take intentional steps to exercise self-control.

Day 27

Seeking Unity in Christ

Scripture Reading: Ephesians 4:3 - "Make every effort to keep the unity of the Spirit through the bond of peace."

PRAYERS : Lord, unite Your people in love and peace. Help us make every effort to foster unity, reflecting the oneness we share in Christ.

Reflection for Spiritual Growth: Reflect on situations where unity may be challenging. How can your actions contribute to maintaining the bond of peace in your relationships?

Daily Challenge and Action: Reach out to someone with whom you may have differences, seeking common ground and understanding.

Day 28

Dwelling in God's Love

Scripture Reading: 1 John 4:16 - "So we have come to know and to believe the love that God has for us. God is love, and anyone who abides in love abides in God, and God abides in them."

PRAYERS : Heavenly Father, help me dwell in Your love. May my life be a reflection of Your love, and may I abide in Your presence.

Reflection for Spiritual Growth: Reflect on the depth of God's love for you. How can abiding in His love transform your perspective and interactions with others?

Daily Challenge and Action: Show love and kindness to those around you, reflecting God's love in your words and actions.

Day 29

Engaging in Acts of Kindness

Scripture Reading: Galatians 6:9-10 - "Let us not become weary in doing good, for at the proper time we will reap a harvest if we do not give up. Therefore, as we have opportunity, let us do good to all people, especially to those who belong to the family of believers."

PRAYERS : Lord, empower me to persist in acts of kindness. May I not grow weary, knowing that in due time, goodness will bear fruit.

Reflection for Spiritual Growth: Reflect on the impact of small acts of kindness. How can cultivating a habit of kindness contribute to your spiritual well-being?

Daily Challenge and Action: Purposefully engage in acts of kindness today, both to those you know and to strangers you encounter.

Day 30

Cultivating a Spirit of Gratitude

Scripture Reading: Colossians 3:15 - "Let the peace of Christ rule in your hearts, since as members of one body you were called to peace. And be thankful."

PRAYERS : Gracious Father, may gratitude rule in my heart. Help me recognize the blessings in my life and cultivate a spirit of thankfulness.

Reflection for Spiritual Growth: Reflect on the importance of gratitude in maintaining inner peace. How can cultivating thankfulness enhance your connection with God?

Daily Challenge and Action: Create a gratitude list, noting down things you are thankful for in your life.

Day 31

Embracing God's Promises

Scripture Reading: 2 Corinthians 1:20 - "For no matter how many promises God has made, they are 'Yes' in Christ. And so through him the 'Amen' is spoken by us to the glory of God."

PRAYERS : Lord, I embrace Your promises. May my life be an 'Amen' to the assurance found in Your Word, bringing glory to Your name.

Reflection for Spiritual Growth: Reflect on the promises of God that resonate with you. How can anchoring your faith in these promises impact your daily walk?

Daily Challenge and Action: Choose a promise from Scripture and meditate on it throughout the day, declaring your 'Amen' to God's faithfulness.

Day 32

Reflecting on God's Faithfulness

Scripture Reading: Lamentations 3:22-23 - "Because of the Lord's great love we are not consumed, for his compassions never fail. They are new every morning; great is your faithfulness."

PRAYERS : Faithful Father, I reflect on Your unwavering love. Your mercies are new every morning, and I trust in Your great faithfulness.

Reflection for Spiritual Growth: Reflect on moments in your life where God's faithfulness has been evident. How can recalling His faithfulness strengthen your trust in Him?

Daily Challenge and Action: Take time to journal or reflect on instances where God has shown His faithfulness in your life.

Day 33

Seeking God's Guidance in Decisions

Scripture Reading: Proverbs 3:5-6 - "Trust in the Lord with all your heart and lean not on your own understanding; in all your ways submit to him, and he will make your paths straight."

PRAYERS : Lord, I trust in Your guidance. Help me surrender my understanding and submit to Your will, confident that You will direct my paths.

Reflection for Spiritual Growth: Reflect on the importance of trusting God's guidance in your decisions. How can relying on His wisdom bring clarity to your choices?

Daily Challenge and Action: Seek God's guidance before making a significant decision today, surrendering your plans to His sovereign will.

Day 34

A Heart of Compassion for the Vulnerable

Scripture Reading: Proverbs 31:8-9 - "Speak up for those who cannot speak for themselves, for the rights of all who are destitute. Speak up and judge fairly; defend the rights of the poor and needy."

PRAYERS : Compassionate Father, may I be an advocate for the vulnerable. Guide me to speak up for those who cannot speak for themselves and defend the rights of the poor.

Reflection for Spiritual Growth: Reflect on ways you can advocate for the vulnerable in your community. How can your actions reflect God's heart for justice?

Daily Challenge and Action: Engage in an act of advocacy or support for a cause that addresses the needs of the vulnerable.

Day 35

Celebrating God's Creation

Scripture Reading: Genesis 1:31 - "God saw all that he had made, and it was very good."

PRAYERS : Creator God, I celebrate Your masterpiece of creation. Open my eyes to see the beauty in the world around me and to appreciate the goodness of Your design.

Reflection for Spiritual Growth: Reflect on the beauty of God's creation. How can appreciating the wonders of nature deepen your awe and gratitude for the Creator?

Daily Challenge and Action: Spend time outdoors today, intentionally appreciating and celebrating the beauty of God's creation.

Day 36

Surrendering Anxieties to God

Scripture Reading: Philippians 4:6-7 - "Do not be anxious about anything, but in every situation, by prayer and petition, with thanksgiving, present your requests to God. And the peace of God, which transcends all understanding, will guard your hearts and your minds in Christ Jesus."

PRAYERS : Heavenly Father, I surrender my anxieties to You. In every situation, I present my requests with thanksgiving, trusting in Your peace that surpasses understanding.

Reflection for Spiritual Growth: Reflect on areas of your life causing anxiety. How can surrendering these concerns to God lead to a deeper experience of His peace?

Daily Challenge and Action: When faced with anxious thoughts today, pause and intentionally present your concerns to God in prayer.

Day 37

Reflecting on God's Mercy

Scripture Reading: Lamentations 3:22-23 - "Because of the Lord's great love we are not consumed, for his compassions never fail. They are new every morning; great is your faithfulness."

PRAYERS : Merciful Father, I reflect on Your unending compassion. Your mercies are new every morning, and I am grateful for Your faithfulness.

Reflection for Spiritual Growth: Reflect on moments when God's mercy has been evident in your life. How can an awareness of His compassion shape your daily perspective?

Daily Challenge and Action: Throughout the day, intentionally pause to acknowledge and give thanks for God's mercy in your life.

Day 38

Nurturing Godly Relationships

Scripture Reading: Ecclesiastes 4:9-10 - "Two are better than one because they have a good return for their labor: If either of them falls down, one can help the other up. But pity anyone who falls and has no one to help them up."

PRAYERS : Lord, guide me in nurturing godly relationships. Help me to be a supportive friend and to surround myself with those who uplift and encourage me in my faith journey.

Reflection for Spiritual Growth: Reflect on the importance of godly relationships in your life. How can intentional connections with fellow believers contribute to your spiritual growth?

Daily Challenge and Action: Reach out to a friend or family member today, offering support, encouragement, or a listening ear.

Day 39

Seeking God's Wisdom in Challenges

Scripture Reading: James 1:5 - "If any of you lacks wisdom, you should ask God, who gives generously to all without finding fault, and it will be given to you."

PRAYERS : Wise Father, grant me Your wisdom. I seek Your guidance in facing challenges, trusting that You generously provide the wisdom needed.

Reflection for Spiritual Growth: Reflect on challenges you are currently facing. How can seeking God's wisdom influence your perspective and actions in difficult situations?

Daily Challenge and Action: Face a challenge today with a prayerful heart, seeking God's wisdom and guidance in your decision-making.

Day 40

Reflecting on the Lenten Journey

Scripture Reading: Psalm 119:105 - "Your word is a lamp for my feet, a light on my path."

PRAYERS : Gracious Lord, as we conclude this Lenten journey, we reflect on the light Your Word has provided. May it continue to guide our steps and illuminate our paths.

Reflection for Spiritual Growth: Reflect on the insights gained and the growth experienced during this Lenten season. How can these lessons shape your ongoing spiritual journey?

Daily Challenge and Action: Take time today to journal or reflect on the key learnings and experiences from this Lenten devotional. Consider how you can continue to apply these insights in your daily life.

Weekly Themes: A Guided Exploration of Lenten Topics

Exploring Weekly Topics

As we embark on this Lenten journey, each week brings a unique theme to delve into, providing a structured and purposeful approach to our reflections and devotions. Let's explore the significance of these weekly themes and how they connect to the overarching Lenten narrative.

Week 1: Renewal and Repentance

Theme: The journey begins with introspection and a call to renewal. We focus on repentance, acknowledging our shortcomings, and seeking God's transformative grace.

Connection to Lenten Themes: This week mirrors the initial phase of Lent, traditionally associated with self-examination and turning away from sin. It lays the foundation for a deeper connection with God.

Week 2: Seeking God's Mercy

Theme: Mercy takes center stage as we reflect on God's compassion and forgiveness. This week invites us to experience the profound mercy that flows from the heart of our loving Creator.

Connection to Lenten Themes: Lent is a season marked by God's mercy and the journey toward redemption. This week aligns with the Lenten call to seek God's forgiveness and embrace His boundless mercy.

Week 3: Embracing Sacrifice and Service

Theme: Sacrifice and service become focal points, encouraging us to emulate Christ's selfless love. This week prompts us to consider how we can live sacrificially and serve others in our daily lives.

Connection to Lenten Themes: Lent, echoing Christ's sacrifice, invites us to reflect on our own acts of self-denial. This week emphasizes the practical outworking of sacrificial love in service to others.

Week 4: Journey of Humility

Theme: Humility takes center stage as we explore the virtues of meekness, considering Christ's humble example. This week encourages us to embrace humility in our relationships and daily interactions.

Connection to Lenten Themes: Lent is a season of humility, where we follow Christ's path of humility and self-emptying. This week calls us to embody Christ's humility in our daily lives.

Week 5: Reflecting on God's Word

Theme: Delving into the richness of God's Word, this week invites us to reflect on Scripture, seeking wisdom and guidance. We explore the transformative power of God's Word in our lives.

Connection to Lenten Themes: Lent is a time of intentional reflection on God's Word, mirroring Jesus' own reliance on Scripture during his time of testing. This week emphasizes the importance of Scripture in our Lenten journey.

Week 6: Cultivating Gratitude

Theme: Gratitude becomes our focus as we reflect on God's goodness and blessings. This week encourages us to develop a heart of thanksgiving, recognizing and appreciating God's abundant grace.

Connection to Lenten Themes: Lent invites us to appreciate the sacrifice of Christ and the grace bestowed upon us. This week emphasizes expressing gratitude as a response to God's love during this season.

Week 7: A Week of Prayerful Silence

Theme: Silence becomes a powerful conduit for prayer and communion with God. This week invites us to embrace moments of quiet reflection, fostering a deeper connection with the Divine.

Connection to Lenten Themes: Lent includes periods of silence and contemplation, mirroring Jesus' time in the wilderness. This week accentuates the significance of silence in enhancing our spiritual intimacy with God.

Week 8: Anticipating Resurrection Hope

Theme: As we approach Easter, this week focuses on the anticipation of resurrection hope. We reflect on the promise of new life in Christ, bringing the Lenten journey to a crescendo of joyous expectation.

Connection to Lenten Themes: Lent ultimately points to the resurrection, the culmination of Christ's redemptive work. This week amplifies our anticipation of the hope and victory found in the resurrection.

Easter Preparation: A Holistic Approach to Resurrection Celebration

Anticipation of Easter Sunday

As we stand on the threshold of Easter Sunday, our hearts are filled with anticipation, echoing the joyous culmination of the Lenten journey. Easter is a celebration of the ultimate victory—Christ's triumph over sin and death. The anticipation is not merely for a historical event but a personal encounter with the risen Savior, a moment of profound transformation and renewed hope.

In the days leading up to Easter Sunday, our anticipation is akin to the dawn breaking after a long night. It's a joyous expectation of the fulfillment of God's promises—a promise of new life, redemption, and eternal joy. As we prepare for Easter, let our anticipation be saturated with gratitude for the sacrificial love of Christ that paved the way for our redemption.

Reflection on Lenten Journey

Easter preparation necessitates a reflective pause, a moment to look back on the Lenten journey traversed. This reflection is not a mere retrospective glance but a deep contemplation of the transformative work God has been orchestrating within our hearts. The Lenten season, marked by repentance, sacrifice, and spiritual disciplines, is a journey toward the Cross—a journey that confronts our brokenness and leads us to the foot of Calvary.

As we reflect on our Lenten journey, let us acknowledge the areas where God's grace has brought healing, the moments of surrender, and the lessons learned through prayer and introspection. The Lenten season is not only a time of personal reflection but also a communal experience of shared repentance and growth. In this reflection, we recognize that Easter's joy is heightened by the profound awareness of the redemptive journey we've traveled.

Spiritual Practices for Holy Week

The Holy Week preceding Easter is a sacred time that invites us to engage in intentional spiritual practices, deepening our connection with the Passion narrative and preparing our hearts for the Resurrection. Here are spiritual practices for each day of Holy Week:

Palm Sunday: Reflection on Christ's Triumphal Entry

Read and meditate on the account of Jesus' triumphal entry into Jerusalem (Matthew 21:1-11). Reflect on the symbolism of the crowd's praise and consider how you honor Christ as your King.
Maundy Thursday: Communion and Footwashing

Participate in a communion service, remembering Jesus' last supper with His disciples.
Consider a symbolic act of humility, such as footwashing, as a reminder of Christ's servant-hearted leadership.
Good Friday: Contemplation of the Cross

Spend time in solemn reflection on the events of Good Friday, particularly Jesus' crucifixion (John 19).

Engage in the Stations of the Cross, contemplating the immense sacrifice made for our redemption.

Holy Saturday: Vigil and Silence

Observe a period of silence and reflection, recognizing the solemnity of Holy Saturday.

Attend an Easter Vigil service if available, focusing on the anticipation of Christ's resurrection.

Easter Sunday: Resurrection Celebration

Begin the day with a joyful Easter sunrise service, celebrating the risen Christ.

Engage in corporate worship, proclaiming the victory of the Resurrection through music and praise.

Reflect on the significance of Christ's triumph over death and the promise of new life.

Easter Sunday: Resurrection Celebration

Significance of Easter Sunday

Easter Sunday stands as the pinnacle of the Christian faith, radiating with the brilliance of the risen Son of God. Its significance is profound and transcendent, marking the victory of Jesus Christ over sin and death. Easter celebrates the foundational truth of Christianity—the resurrection of Jesus from the tomb, validating His identity as the Messiah and offering the hope of eternal life to all who believe.

The significance of Easter Sunday lies in the transformative power of the resurrection. It is the moment when darkness surrenders to light, despair yields to hope, and death is conquered by life. The empty tomb is not just a historical event; it is a living testimony to God's redemptive plan and His boundless love for humanity. Easter Sunday, therefore, is a celebration of the core tenet of Christianity—the resurrection of Jesus Christ, bringing salvation and everlasting joy to all who embrace Him as Lord and Savior.

Joyful Reflections

The atmosphere of Easter Sunday is infused with uncontainable joy—a joy that emanates from the realization that death could not hold Jesus captive. It's a joy that permeates the deepest corners of our hearts, dispelling sorrow and infusing our lives with hope. As we celebrate the resurrection, our reflections are laced with gratitude, awe, and an overwhelming sense of God's grace.

We reflect joyfully on the victory won on Calvary's hill, where Jesus triumphed over sin and death. The resurrection is a source of perpetual joy, reminding us that, in Christ, every ending is a prelude to a glorious new beginning. Our reflections on Easter Sunday are not just retrospective; they are a jubilant affirmation of the present reality that we serve a risen and living Savior.

Easter Scripture Readings and Prayers

Scripture Readings:

Matthew 28:1-10: The angel's proclamation of the empty tomb and Jesus' victory over death.
1 Corinthians 15:20-22: Paul's affirmation of Christ's resurrection as the firstfruits of those who have fallen asleep.
John 20:11-18: Mary Magdalene's encounter with the risen Jesus, illustrating the personal and transformative nature of the resurrection.
Prayers:

Opening Prayer:
Heavenly Father, as we gather on this glorious Easter Sunday, our hearts overflow with gratitude for the resurrection of Your Son, Jesus Christ. May the joy of His victory fill our souls, and may our worship be a fragrant offering of praise to the Risen King.

Prayer of Thanksgiving:
Lord Jesus, we thank You for conquering sin and death through Your resurrection. In this season of

celebration, we lift our voices in grateful praise for the hope and life You have secured for us. Your victory is our joy, and Your grace is our everlasting song.

Prayer of Renewal:
Holy Spirit, renew our hearts on this Easter Sunday. May the truth of the resurrection inspire us to live as resurrected people, transformed by the power of Christ's love. Empower us to walk in the newness of life that Your resurrection brings.

Closing Prayer:
Lord, as we leave this place of celebration, may the reality of the empty tomb resonate in our daily lives. May the joy of Easter Sunday be a constant source of strength, assurance, and hope. In the name of the risen Jesus, we pray. Amen.

Easter Sunday, with its significance, joyful reflections, and Scripture readings, is a day of exuberant worship and profound gratitude. It is a time to rejoice in the resurrection power that continues to transform lives and offer the hope of eternal glory to all who believe.

As we draw the final curtain on this sacred journey through the pages of the "3-Minute Lent Daily Devotional 2024," let our hearts echo with the profound melodies of redemption and grace. This book has been more than a guide; it has been a companion on the pilgrimage of the soul, weaving together the threads of repentance, sacrifice, and resurrection hope.

In the depth of our reflections, each word, each prayer, and every moment of contemplation has been a brushstroke painting a portrait of a deeper connection with the Divine. As we part ways with these pages, may the resonance of the Lenten journey linger in the recesses of our spirits, a gentle reminder of the transformative power of God's love.

The reflections penned within these chapters are not mere ink on paper; they are whispers of grace, beckoning us to live in the light of the risen Son. The story of Lent is not confined to the constraints of time or the boundaries of this book; it's a narrative that transcends, inviting us to carry the lessons learned into the tapestry of our daily lives.

As the final chapter unfolds, let gratitude well up within us, for in every word, in every scripture, and in every prayer, we have encountered the living Christ. May the fragrance of this Lenten devotional linger as a reminder that our journey with Christ is not confined to forty days but extends into the eternity of His unfailing love.

Made in the USA
Columbia, SC
26 January 2024